Genre Expository Text

P9-DXL-762

Essential Question
How does the earth change?

EARTHQUAKES

by Elizabeth Doering

Chapter 1

Earthquakes

Imagine this. You are sitting at home. It is a nice day. Then the house shakes. Dishes rattle. A hanging lamp sways. What is happening? You are not sure. It could be an earthquake.

A serious earthquake struck San Francisco, California, in 1989.

firemen

Roger Ressmeyer/Corbis

building

China was hit hard by an earthquake in 2010.

Strong earthquakes are big news. But there were earthquakes a long time ago, too. People did not know much about them. They did not understand earthquakes.

We know more about earthquakes now. There was an earthquake in Virginia during the summer of 2011. Many people living on the East Coast felt it.

> **In Other Words** Eastern region of the United States. En español: *la costa esta.*

The map shows the effects of the 2011 quake.

Understanding the Map
The star shows the center of the earthquake.
The circles show where people felt it.

Illustration: Rob Schuster

A strong earthquake hit Japan in March 2011. Japan's main island moved 8 feet (2.4 meters). This earthquake even moved Earth on its **axis**!

There are many earthquakes in Japan.

crack

Earthquakes happen most often near places called fault lines. Fault lines are deep cracks in the ground. There is an active fault in California. It is called the San Andreas fault.

Language Detective | Is is a helping verb. Find another helping verb on page 2.

The fault runs along most of California.

fault

Robert E. Wallace/U.S. Geological Survey

river island

The Mississippi River is over 2,300 miles long.

Earthquakes can affect large areas of land. This happened near the Mississippi River in 1811 and 1812. Big earthquakes hit the area. They created huge waves in the river and landslides on hills. The land moved up and down. Steep cracks opened up in the ground!

STOP AND CHECK

What have you learned about earthquakes so far?

Chapter 2

What Causes Earthquakes?

Earth's surface has strange properties. It seems like one solid piece. But its crust is actually made of broken pieces. These are called **plates.**

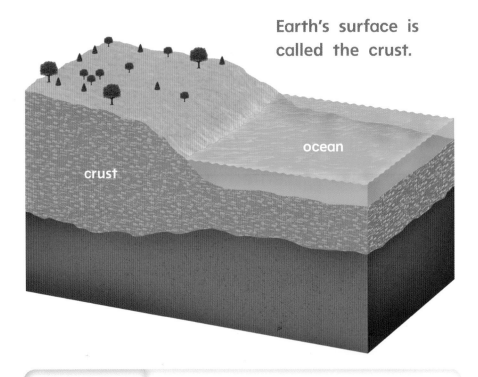

Earth's surface is called the crust.

ocean

crust

Illustration: Rob Schuster

Language Detective	Earth's is a possessive noun. Find another possessive noun on page 5.

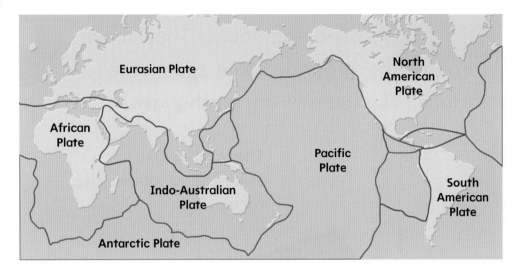

Earthquakes usually happen near where two plates meet. The lines show the outlines of the plates.

Plates

Plates move very slowly. Sometimes they slide past each other. Sometimes plates pull away from each other. This can make rocks underground explode. When the rocks break, it can cause shock waves.

Shock Waves

Shock waves begin deep underground at a point called the focus. They move through the ground. Some reach the surface. This causes an earthquake.

The earthquake's epicenter is above the focus.

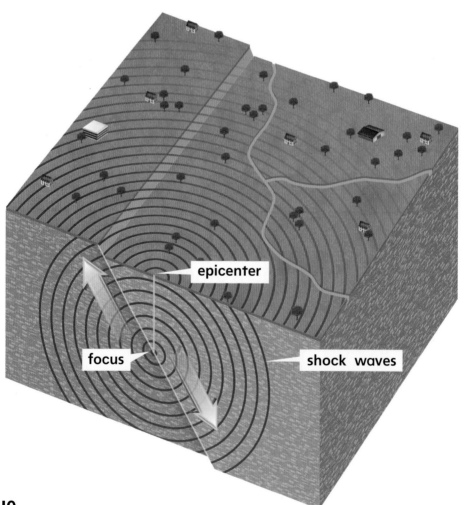

epicenter

focus

shock waves

Illustration: Rob Schuster

The earthquake is most powerful at the epicenter. It is less strong farther away from the epicenter.

Earthquakes happen under the ocean, too. These cause waves called **tsunami**.

Tsunami are giant waves that hit the shore.

boat

debris

Tsunami

Tsunami waves start small. They get bigger as they get closer to land. Some of these waves can grow as tall as a ten-story building! They suck up all the water near the shore. Then they crash down on land.

This is what a tsunami looks like as it grows.

tsunami

Rod Haestier/Alamy

STOP AND CHECK

What causes shock waves?

seismograph

scientist

This machine tells how strong an earthquake is.

Measuring Earthquakes

Some earthquakes are big, but most earthquakes are small. Scientists use many different tools to study earthquakes. One machine is called a **seismograph.** It tells the local **magnitude**. This is how strong an earthquake is at a certain place.

Earthquakes are part of nature. They will keep happening. But we know a lot more about earthquakes now than we did in the past. This makes life safer for people who live in places where earthquakes happen.

Seismographs looked different in the past. This seismograph was used in ancient China.

Respond to Reading

Summarize

Use important details to help you summarize *Earthquakes*.

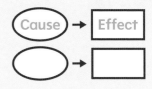

Text Evidence

1. How do you know *Earthquakes* is expository text? Genre

2. What kind of waves are caused by earthquakes under the ocean? Cause and Effect

3. Use sentence clues to figure out the meaning of *sways* on page 2. Sentence Clues

4. Write about why earthquakes happen. Write About Reading

Compare Texts
Read to find out how glaciers change Earth.

Glaciers

Glaciers are huge masses of ice, snow, rock, and water that form on mountains. The tops of mountains get a lot of snow. The snow piles up in layers. This causes ice to form under the top layer. Soon the ice starts to slide down the mountain. The glacier slowly begins to move.

glacier

mountain

Some glaciers look blue.

Ingram Publishing/SuperStock

Rivers of Ice

Glaciers are like rivers of ice. They do not stay still. They flow. Glaciers can change the landscape as they move.

glacier

This glacier in Alaska is crumbling.

There are glaciers everywhere, even near the equator. The equator is warm. But the glaciers are up high in the mountains. It is much cooler there.

glacier

elephant

The glacier on top of Mount Kilimanjaro in Tanzania, Africa, is melting.

Fuse/Getty Images

Melting Glaciers

Warm temperatures may cause glaciers to melt. Glaciers contain most of the fresh water in the world. What would happen if that ice melted?

Make Connections

How do earthquakes change Earth?
Essential Question

How are glaciers like tsunami? How are they different? Text to Text

Glossary

axis an imaginary line around which Earth rotates *(page 5)*

magnitude amount or size *(page 13)*

plates very large sheets of rock that form part of Earth's surface *(page 8)*

seismograph a machine that measures and records earthquakes *(page 13)*

tsunami a huge ocean wave that hits shore *(pages 11)*

Index

Focus on Science

Purpose To make a model of how earthquakes change Earth's surface

What to Do

Step 1 You'll need a pencil, a bake pan, two pieces of fabric, wet soil, and toy trees, houses, or people.

Step 2 Place fabric pieces in pan. Leave ends hanging out. Fill pan with soil. Pat it down. Use your pencil to make a path in the middle.

Step 3 Place toys on top of soil. Grab the ends of the fabric pieces. Pull hard in opposite directions.

Conclusion Write a few sentences about the results. How is this like an earthquake?